MATTHEW EARNEST

I, Ca$$ie...

or

The end of days

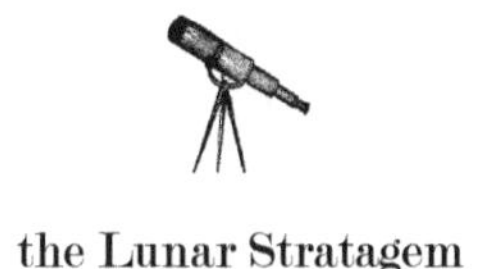

the Lunar Stratagem

I, Ca$$ie... or The end of days had its world premiere on January 12, 2012 at The Joan C. Edwards Performing Arts Center at Marshall University, Huntington, WV. It was written and directed by Matthew Earnest, performed by Nicole Perrone, and designed by William Bezek (Scenery, Costume, and Props), James Kosmatka (Sound), and Matthew Earnest (Lights). Stage Manager was Shelby Brewster.

The piece was subsequently presented at English Theater Berlin, March 20-24, 2012.

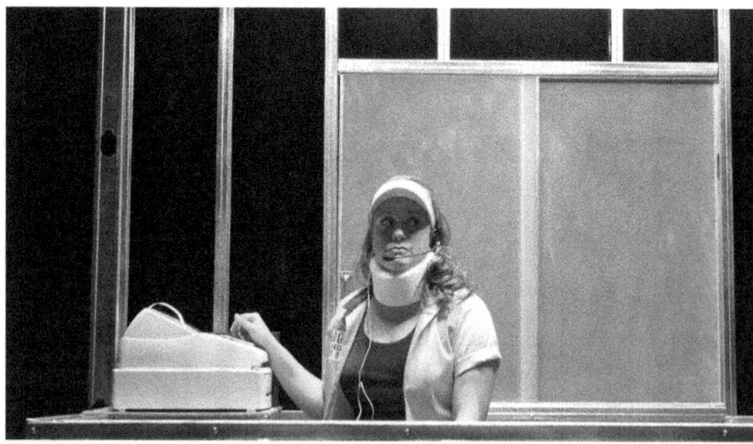

I, Ca$$ie... or The end of days

ISBN 978-0-615-59699-0

All photos of Nicole Perrone as Ca$$ie by William Bezek, except pp. 27, 38 & 44 by Sholten Singer, courtesy of *The Herald-Dispatch*.

Information: The Lunar Stratagem
P.O. Box 574
Huntington, WV 25710

ACKNOWLEDGMENTS

Thank you Dr. Julie Jackson, Chair, & the students, faculty, and staff of the Marshall University Department of Theatre for your enthusiasm and efforts; and thank you Donald Van Horn, Dean, & the Marshall University College of Fine Arts.

Thanks to Jamez-Morris Smith, Deb Carder-Deem, and Kevin Bannon for your invaluable technical expertise and love of theater.

Thanks to the actors who voiced the callers and drive-thru customers in the piece: Kellie Bean, Shelby Brewster, Jack Cirillo, Samuel Kincaid, Michael Mauldin, Ethan Treutle, and Mary Williams.

Thank you to the board members of the Lunar Stratagem. Thank you Doreen & Garth McBride, and Cord Coen. And thanks to my favorite Western Civ professor and theater enthusiast, Dr. Mel Earnest.

And my most special thanks to my oldest and dearest friend, Candace Johnson Lynch, who gave me a quiet place to write.

M.E.

SCENE ONE: Drive-thru

(CA$$IE IS A VERY PRETTY TEENAGER. SHE WEARS A UNIFORM AND MATCHING VISOR. SHE STANDS AT HER REGISTER AND SPEAKS INTO A HEADSET MICROPHONE. SHE MULTI-TASKS: THE EARPIECE FOR THE HEADSET IS IN ONE OF HER EARS, AND THE EARPIECE FOR HER CELLPHONE IS IN THE OTHER.)

CA$$IE

(AFFECTING A MASCULINE VOICE:) *"Why aren't you crying?"*

(PAUSE.)

I was like... "Excuse me?"

(AGAIN:) *"Why. Aren't. You. CRYING?!"*

He was, I don't know, some creeper in a suit, kinda old, like, I don't know, maybe 40. And I was like, "Cry for what?" But he just kept saying, *"Cry-y-y-y-y! Cry-y-y-y-y-y! CRY!!"*, straight-up screaming really, like some swizzleheaded street person, looking at me like something was my fault.

APHRA ON THE PHONE

Omigod, Ca$$ie!

CA$$IE

Riiiiight?? OK: 1. Inappropriate. 2. Awkward. 3. REEELLY scary. So I was like "I'm out," and I just turned and bolted without my coffee and Helen was with me and she didn't realize at first that I was leaving, like maybe I was just going to the bathroom or something. Actually, I don't know what the hell she thought, but when she finally got it she came running after me all freaked out and by the time she caught up I was halfway down the frigging block, running for my frigging life practically! I mean why do people even speak to you in public? I don't get it. AT. ALL. I mean I'm in line for coffee like every good citizen or whatever, and some retard wants to spew a load of crazy all over me? Like it's my fault his wife hates him and his daughter's pregnant and he just lost his job or what-the-hell-ever. You know?

APHRA ON THE PHONE

Tooootally.

CA$$IE

(SHIVERS.) Ew!

APHRA ON THE PHONE

Omigod, Ca$$ie!

CA$$IE

Have you ever heard of anything so random?

APHRA ON THE PHONE

Omigod, Ca$$ie!

CA$$IE

So fucked up.

APHRA ON THE PHONE

Tooootally.

CA$$IE

And as a result of the actions of said retard, Ca$$ie goes to school without her coffee this morning. (GIVES A QUICK, BRIGHT SMILE!) Do I need to remind you that that very thing has in the past had extremely tragic consequences? This in addition to the news that my *adorable*, and according to my parents, BRILLIANT, PERFECT, BRILLIANT, LIGHT-OF-THE-WORLD little brother Hector and his stupid friends snuck into my closet last week when I was outside in the backyard on the phone, got into my stuff, and read my freaking journals!, (God knows what they've told everyone – they've probably already revealed every intimate secret I ever had about *everything* and wrote my phone number on every boys' bathroom wall in town. They're like a Greek chorus of creepy little freshmen with acne and sweaty palms. Ech!). AND, my parents are treating me like a leper from Ethiopia because of what happened last week. Barely speaking to me, even. (PAUSE.) They're upset. About Hector. (PAUSE.) I mean *Shit*, Aphra. When I go to college next year, why don't I just major in grief and humiliation? Perfect! (DEEP BREATH.) So whatcha doin?

(**SOUND**: BEEP OR OTHER ELECTRONIC INDICATOR THAT SOMEONE IS AT THE DRIVE-THRU.)

CA$$IE

Wait, hold on a second. Welcome to Bigger Burger, order whenever you're ready. (PAUSE.) Hello?

MUFFLED MALE VOICE

Yes, I'm here. Not sure what I want yet.

CA$$IE

Order whenever you're ready, sir. (INTO PHONE.) Aphra?

APHRA ON THE PHONE

Ca$$ie?

CA$$IE
Just a second. Some dude doesn't know what he wants.

(PAUSE.)

MUFFLED MALE VOICE
Uh, hello?

CA$$IE
Yes, yes, I'm here, sir. Order whenever you're ready.

MUFFLED MALE VOICE
Yeah, uh, what's the #12?

CA$$IE
That would be a tepid, artificial meat sandwich made from genetically altered animals.

MUFFLED MALE VOICE
(BEAT.) I beg your pardon?

CA$$IE
Yes, every single ingredient has been fabricated in a lab in the Midwest by scientists who make 2,017 times the salary of the average worker who serves their creations here at Bigger Burger.

MUFFLED MALE VOICE
O...K...??

CA$$IE
It comes with a side of frozen starch fried to annihilation in synthetic oils and slathered in condiments you'll never be able to digest. It has no natural components, is full of artificial dyes, and has absolutely no nutritional value whatsoever.

(PAUSE.)

MUFFLED MALE VOICE
Uh, OK. I'll take a #12 with a Coke, please.

CA$$IE
Would you like to *Max It Out!* for an extra $2.73?

MUFFLED MALE VOICE
Uh, sure.

CA$$IE
Any dessert tonight? The frozen log flume is $1 for a limited time only.

MUFFLED MALE VOICE
What's that?

CA$$IE
The flume? O, it's uh… it's a log. It's a brown log.

(PAUSE.)

MUFFLED MALE VOICE
Sure, I'll take one.

CA$$IE
One flume… Your total is $7.61. Please drive through to the second window.

(**SOUND**: CA$$IE'S PHONE RINGS. HER RINGTONE IS THE CHORUS OF *Blow* BY KE$HA. SHE ANSWERS THE PHONE IMMEDIATELY.)

CA$$IE
Aphra? Did you hang up?

APHRA ON THE PHONE
Ca$$ie?

CA$$IE

Hey. So welcome to today's episode of my own personal hell, starring yours truly, Ca$$ie the confused, no, the *confined.* Ca$$ie the freakin *confined.* I mean, somebody please just pour gasoline on my life and strike a match.

APHRA ON THE PHONE

Omigod, Ca$$ie!

CA$$IE

Pfff, you have no idea. I mean they handcuffed me, Aphra. THEY. HAND. CUFFED. ME. (!) Do you have any clue what that's like? OK, picture this: Your parents, the people who actually gave you life, have built more than half the freakin city we live in and are on every single board in town. If Troy had a king and queen instead of a dumb-ass mayor, it'd be them. Every bum in every soup kitchen, every little girl in every dance class at the Y, every student in every new building at the university, everyone who walks in the parks, visits the hospital, goes to the symphony, all of them, ALL of them depend on, and are furthermore and understandably grateful for the largesse of your parents. Troy would be pretty friggin bereft and hopeless without them, frankly. Now this is not even mentioning your long and unimpeachable family history – generations of savvy entrepreneurs, industrialists, professionals, inventive capitalists, *etc.*, who dug canals, created systems for production, built factories and plants, employed thousands of people, fed thousands of families and put this damn place on the map, for Christ's sake. No, don't even mention that, please. Let's just talk about your parents right now. Your parents. (SIGH. PAUSE.)

Your parents had to go down to the police station with coats on over their pajamas and bail you out of frigging jail.

Tragic. And absurd! Like, who *wasn't* drinking that night? What? It's my last homecoming game, I'm a frigging senior for God's sake (and P.S.: everybody EVERYBODY knew I was gonna get Homecoming Queen, the first time in the history of Troy High School, by the way, that the valedictorian and Homecoming Queen will be the same person, OK? I mean, I know you already knew that. I just have to repeat it because it's part of what makes this whole thing such a flaming debacle of nonsense.), and what?... *I'm not supposed to drink at the game???* Interesting! Don't tell me Alexander wasn't drunk that night – yeah, Alexander, the beautiful and verrrry gay son of the very man who hauled me in like some sex offender or drug dealer. Like I'm a criminal or something. Like I'm not normal. Hey! Newsflash: EVERYBODY HAS CAR ACCIDENTS FROM TIME TO TIME. I mean, Aphra... for real? Me? Sitting in the backseat of a squad car? HaHaa! So yeah, here I am, living in a warped version of purgatory that would make even Dante shudder and flee. Total epic surreal fuck-up. I mean *Christ*:

"Two months of community service at a local business."

What? Like, my parents used to own the land this stupid joint sits on, and Lo!, here's their daughter, clad entirely in the finest polyester, dispensing engineered misery in a bag to the disenfranchised and oblivious who can't afford to eat anything else. Uchh! I seriously hate my life right now. And guess who's cheering at the game tonight in my place: Who do you think? Frigging *Pandora*. Fat frigging cow.

(OPENS THE WINDOW. TO THE MAN IN THE CAR, WITH A SMILE:) $7.61. (SHE TAKES THE MONEY, HANDS HIM THE BAG, SHUTS THE WINDOW.) And the only reason she's even cheering this year is because she's MY friend. I mean, you can just look at her and see that *nobody's* gonna be lifting her over their head any time soon. But if by some miracle she gets tossed in the air tonight they'd better not frigging drop her, cause if she hits the ground her tonnage will push right on through to the core of the earth and cause all the world's volcanoes to erupt simultaneously so the planet will choke on its own vomit and implode. (BEAT.) Sorry, but that's just the truth. And guess what: they won't even let me *study* here! I mean, Hello! I'm young! Isn't it obvious that I'm a student? (LOOKS AROUND FURTIVELY. SPEAKS IN A SLIGHTLY LOWER TONE.) I have to be quiet because the manager's still here somewhere, but Jesus, Aphra! How's it gonna look if I fuck off my last semester of high school? Two months' of this drive-thru shit with no studying? What, are they trying to sabotage my life in the most epic, despicable way possible??? Cute! You know I've had a 4.0 basically since the day I started kindergarten, won medals in track and volleyball, went to state for speech and debate, sang in the chorale all four years, cheerleading captain, aced all the college entrance exams, and now valedictorian AND frigging Homecoming Queen! APHRA: I'VE ALREADY HAD TEA WITH RECRUITERS FROM ALL THE BEST SCHOOLS!, and now what? It's my senior year, and I'm shoved into a hole like a veal calf, not even allowed to work on my history homework or whatever? What's gonna happen to me? Omigod, Aphra. My dad will seriously stroke out and disown me if I don't get into a good school. (BREATHES DEEPLY.) I need to calm down. (WHIMPERS.) *I'm seriously freaking out here!*

APHRA ON THE PHONE

Omigod, Ca$$ie!

CA$$IE

(SIGH.) Fuck. Maybe if I just take a hot shower and bury myself in bed, this entire nightmare will be over when I wake up tomorrow morning, and I can go back to my life. A new frigging day will dawn, and I can just start over. (PAUSE.) Do I even have time to start over?

(**SOUND**: BEEP OR OTHER ELECTRONIC INDICATOR THAT SOMEONE IS AT THE DRIVE-THRU.)

CA$$IE

(INTO PHONE:) Hold on. (INTO HEADSET MIC:) Welcome to Bigger Burger, order whenever you're ready. (PAUSE.) Hello?

OLDER WOMAN AT DRIVE-THRU

Yes. Er..., hello?

CA$$IE

Order whenever you're ready. (INTO PHONE.) Aphra?

APHRA ON THE PHONE

Ca$$ie?

CA$$IE

So last night I went to Food Plus and bought tampons. I got them home and they had CARDBOARD FUCKING APPLICATORS. Just kill me.

OLDER WOMAN AT DRIVE-THRU

Hello?

CA$$IE
Yes, ma'am, order whenever you're ready.

OLDER WOMAN AT DRIVE-THRU
Are you... Are you hiring, right now? I'd like to... Well, I'd like to fill out an application. For a job.

(PAUSE.)

...Hello?

CA$$IE
Um... I'm not sure, ma'am... (PAUSE. CA$$IE IS VERY UNCOMFORTABLE.)

CA$$IE
Could you come back in an hour and speak to the manager?

OLDER WOMAN AT DRIVE-THRU
Yes, yes, I suppose I can. I just... (MUFFLED SPEECH.) ...out of work for so long. I... (BEGINS TO CRY.) I'm sorry. I'm so sorry. Thank you. (**SOUND**: THROUGH CA$$IE'S HEADSET, A RUNDOWN CAR PULLING AWAY. SILENCE.)

CA$$IE
(*What just happened?*) (**LIGHTS**: CHANGE.)

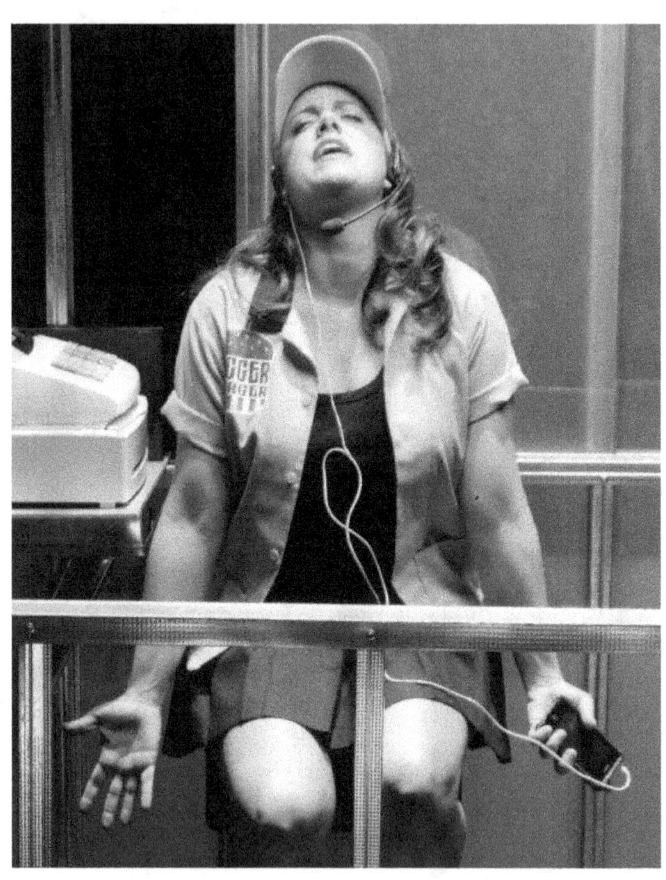

SCENE 2: DUI

(CA$$IE PERFORMS AN ELABORATE CHEER ROUTINE USING THE ALCOHOL PENAL CODE. SHE CHEERS.)

CA$$IE

Driving Under the Influence: Minors!: Section 106.041 of the Penal Code / makes it illegal / for a minor / to operate a motor vehicle in a public / place while having any detectable amount of alcohol in the minor's / system.

Driving under the influence / is a Class C misdemeanor / punishable by a fine / an alcohol awareness course / community service / and driver's license suspension! Woo-hoo!

Driving While Intoxicated with an Open Container: Section 49.04 states that driving / while intoxicated / with an open container of alcohol in the person's / immediate possession / is a Class B misdemeanor / with a minimum term of confinement / of six / days.

Definition / of Intoxication / Chapter 49.01 / Section (2)(a). Quote: "Not having the normal use / of mental or physical faculties / by reason of the introduction / of alcohol / a controlled substance / a drug (PAUSE.) a combination of those substances / or any other substance into the body. OR having a blood/alcohol concentration of .05? Nope. .06? Uh-uh. .07? Pshhh...

.08 or more! Woo-hoo!!

(**SOUND**: MARCHING BAND PLAYS FIGHT SONG. **LIGHTS**: CHANGE.)

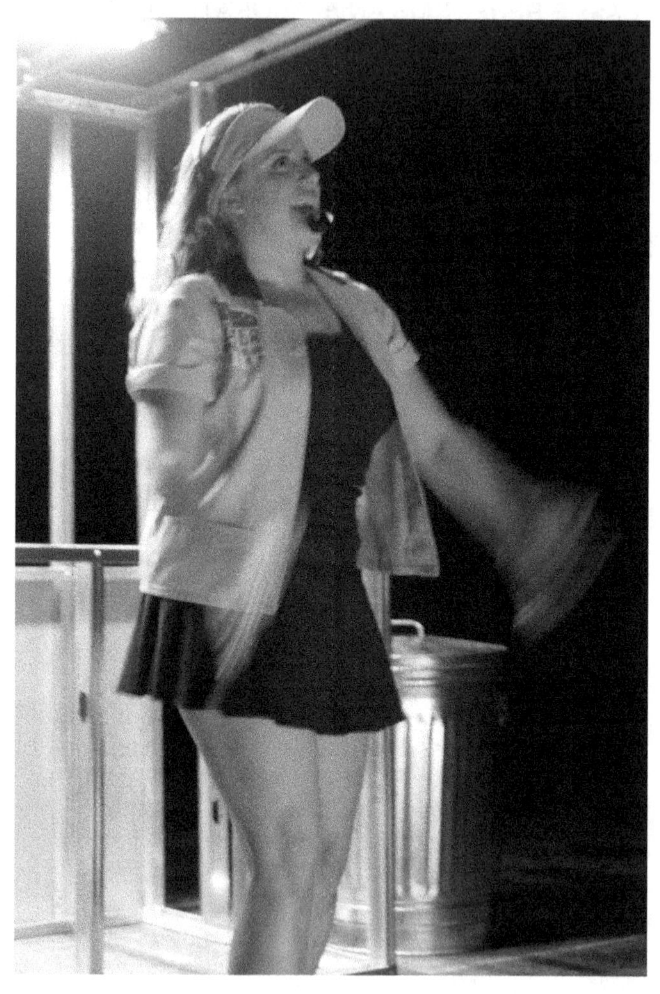

SCENE 3: *Western Civ*

(LATER.)

APHRA ON THE PHONE

Ca$$ie?

CA$$IE

Yeah, yeah. (BEAT.) So what's with *Western Civ*? I mean, what's with the new Western Civ *teacher*? Does he really expect us to take that exam on Friday, cuz I've got news for him: if I just hiked up my skirt and pissed on it I'd probably get a better grade. Why, you ask? Oh, let's see, maybe because *I'm used to being frigging taught something before I'm tested over the frigging material!!* Revolutionary, I know. And what happened to Apollo, anyway? It's really a pain in the ass when a teacher leaves mid-semester, but then why would they consider the students' side of it? We're only the ones whose parents' *considerable* tax money pays their salaries.

Western Civilization. Ha! What a sick fucking joke.

Dr. Apollo was stupid, but at least he was consistent. I wonder what happened to him. Maybe he got married. Nah. Ooh! Maybe he fell prey to the dreaded *Raubwirtschaft*.

APHRA ON THE PHONE

Toootally.

CA$$IE

Hahaha! Swear to God, if I heard him say *Raubwirtschaft* one more time I was gonna launch my mechanical pencil point-first into his toad-like eyeball! Finally, one day I raised my hand and I was like, "We get it! The Roman economy was based on colonialism and plundering other countries for resources, and since the government invested no monies in the outlying provincial lands they plundered, and since the whole thing had been built on slave labor anyway, it was all smoke and mirrors, completely unsustainable. It was just a matter of time until it all fell apart, right? Not to mention all the failed military escapades of tiny-dick generals and debauched emperors trying to leave 'legacies' or some shit."

CA$$IE as DR. APOLLO

"*Raubwirtschaft*" is much more complicated, Cassandra.

CA$$IE

"But, it happens all the time, right? It's like, business as usual, as far as I can tell from our textbook. Like mergers and acquisitions on a grand scale, but with bullets instead of signatures. And the idea that it's unethical is fairly modern. In fact, I can't find a single mention of the term prior to the 19th century with the scramble to colonize Africa, which would have coincided directly with the very same sentimental Victoriana that gave the world Tennyson and table skirts. And really, Apollo, isn't 'Imperialism' followed by 'Collapse' the way it's supposed to go? It's natural. It's like, human nature. Not to mention, and I mean this in a strictly anthropological sense with no pejorative implication whatsoever, but would the Africans even have a *wheel* if Western powers hadn't gone down there looking for platinum or diamonds or whatever? Seriously. I think there's a philanthropic angle to Imperialism that nobody seems to have the balls to discuss.

CA$$IE as DR. APOLLO

"*Raubwirtschaft*" is rape on a large scale, Cassandra. Pure and simple.

CA$$IE

And I was like, "Whoa... Borderline inappropriate. I thought this was a *Western Civ* class." Apollo totally wanted in my pants too, so obvious. (Everybody knows he picks out a new girl every year to suffocate with attention and shower with A-plusses, usually a brunette.) And he was *obsessed* with the Romans. OB. SESSED! Probably some kinda toga fetish or something. He spent so much time on the Romans I knew we'd never get through the rest of the book, so I was like *whateverwhatever,* screw it. I'll use this excruciatingly long hour and sixteen minutes every day to paint my nails and do homework for other classes.

Raubwirtschaft. Ugh. I am sooo over the past! I'm so bored with *thee* and *thou!* Enough already! When do we get to talk about US, about what's happening *right now*, *today?* Or about what might be happening tomorrow – the future! Hm, maybe we should be talking about *that*, ya think? Uchh, somebody bring me a vicodin *stat!*

APHRA ON THE PHONE

Tooootally.

CA$$IE

And hey, Apollo, your very subtle implication that we're anything remotely like the Romans is faulty logic, because guess what? We don't have slavery anymore! We did like, forever ago, but today? No slavery! People get *paid* to work nowadays!

(**SOUND**: BEEP OR OTHER ELECTRONIC INDICATOR THAT SOMEONE IS AT THE DRIVE-THRU.)

CA$$IE

(INTO PHONE:) Hold on, Aphra. (INTO HEADSET MIC:) Welcome to Bigger Burger, order whenever you're ready. (**SOUND**: HORSE WHINNY.) Hello? (**SOUND**: HORSE RUNS AWAY. INTO PHONE, SLIGHTLY FREAKED OUT.) Aphra?

APHRA ON THE PHONE

Ca$$ie?

CA$$IE

Yeah, so what's going on this weekend? Please tell me all about what you're doing so I can be *ultra*-humiliated by the fact that I'm under house frigging arrest. O, did I mention that I have to wear an ankle bracelet? O yeah. It's *über*-attractive: about 30 pounds of cold steel and plastic tourniquet crunching the ankle I twisted last week at the game. Funsies! Yeah, this is the life I'm living these days. I guess the good constables of Troy are afraid I'll skip town and wreck other cars in other towns far away from here, so they want to make sure they know exactly where this *very* dangerous criminal is at all times of day and night. (MAKES A SCARY FACE.) *Oooooh!* Yeah, so please, tell me all about how you're going to the movies with your Adonis tonight and about how you'll probably meet up with everybody afterwards because Penny's parents are out of town and it's still warm enough to swim and you'll all jump in drunk and laugh all night with fat fucking Pandora who needs lipo and rhinoplasty like *yesterday*. *Please!* tell me all about it, *Aphra!*, cuz *I'm about to pull a Timothy McVeigh and trash this whole fucking place and dance out into the night with nothing but the polyester on my back! Seriously!!* (PANICKING.)

Aphra?

Aphra!

(PAUSE. SHE THROWS THE PHONE DOWN.)

Ughhhh!!

(PAUSE. **SOUND**: PHONE RINGS. CA$$IE PUSHES THE DECLINE BUTTON, THROWS PHONE DOWN AGAIN.)

Stupid bitch.

(PAUSE. PICKS PHONE BACK UP, DIALS. **SOUND**: WE HEAR IT RING IN HER EAR BUD. **SOUND**: A CLICK AS CA$$IE'S MOTHER, HECUBA, ANSWERS THE CALL.)

HECUBA ON THE PHONE

(HEARTBROKEN.) Hi, honey.

CA$$IE

Hey mom whatcha doin?

HECUBA ON THE PHONE

O... nothing, honey.

(PAUSE.)

CA$$IE

Are you still there?

Mom, this is ridiculous. I have to study tonight! Please can you do something? Mom?

(SILENCE.)

Mom, he's gonna be OK.

HECUBA ON THE PHONE

O, honey.

CA$$IE

Mom, look, the doctor said they see those kinds of injuries all the time and that he has a really good chance of being 100% totally perfectly OK. (SILENCE.)

((*Mommy?*))

He's gonna be OK!

HECUBA ON THE PHONE

O, honey.

CA$$IE

I didn't mean to hurt anybody, especially Hector! How many times do I have to apologize? And to *you* of all people! You're supposed to have my back no matter what. *Christ, Mom!* The girls all walked away with just scratches! Except Iris, I mean. But she's only gonna be in a cast for a while. Jeez, it's not like she went through the windshield or anything horrible!

(PAUSE.)

I'm gonna pay you and Dad back for my car. Every cent. I swear I will, Mom. I swear to you.

(PAUSE.)

Mom! You're treating me like a criminal! God!, what did I ever do to *you*? I mean, why don't you just waterboard me? It'd be a hell of a lot better than this blistering silent treatment. The thing you guys don't seem to grasp is that it was an ACCIDENT! I didn't mean to hurt anybody. I. DIDN'T. MEAN. TO. HURT. HECTOR! Doesn't that matter? Does it count for anything with you? I didn't. Mean. To do it. Everybody drinks in high school, Mom. (INTENTIONALLY NASTY.) I'm sure you did too.

(SILENCE.)

Listen, I'm not gonna be able to do this probation thing, at least not like this, absolutely no way I'm gonna be able to do this, so I suggest you and Dad make a call and get me out of here because the alternative is that I'm just gonna walk out and then we'll *all* be in real trouble. *Mom!, I've got to study tonight!* It's my whole future on the line here! Do you want me to fail *Western Civ* and *World History* and lose all my offers from those schools? Is that what you're gunning for here, Mom? Cause that's where all this is headed, and I gotta tell you it scares the crap outta me. What'll happen to me then? (STARTS TO FAKE CRY.) I don't know how to do this job. I can't do it. I've tried, Mom. They're all terrible to me, they treat me like shit, and I have to study. I have to study NOW, Mom. Would you please help me?

MOM!!!

(SILENCE. **SOUND**: THE CALL IS DISCONNECTED.)

Great. Hung up on by my own frigging mother. Yay. (**SOUND**: CA$$IE'S PHONE RINGS AGAIN. SHE ANSWERS.) Hey, Aphra, what's up?

APHRA ON THE PHONE

Ca$$ie?

CA$$IE

Hey, if you bring me a Caesar I'll be your best friend. A small one, no croutons. I'm frigging starving and I'm covered – I mean *covered* with grease, or whatever it is they're using to fry three tons of food products a day here. (SHIVERS.) Ew. I think I'm breathing it. It's in my lungs like cancer or... *maggots*. I'll probably go into renal failure and have an aneurism, and tomorrow some janitor will find me here stiff as a board in this dreary uniform with the left side of my face hanging down like melted wax in the drive-thru window of Bigger frigging Burger. Jesus, Buddha, Krishna, whoever!, please just smite me into a permanent vegetative coma so at least I won't be conscious of my pathetic fate here in this disposable building. Please! O God! You know... Hector is actually really, really lucky right now that he doesn't have to be awake to see his sister languishing in this greasy torture chamber of depravity and hopelessness... Aphra?

APHRA ON THE PHONE

Ca$$ie?

CA$$IE

Can you bring me a Caesar?

APHRA ON THE PHONE

Toootally

CA$$IE

K, thanks. (HANGS UP THE PHONE.)

(**LIGHTS**: CHANGE.)

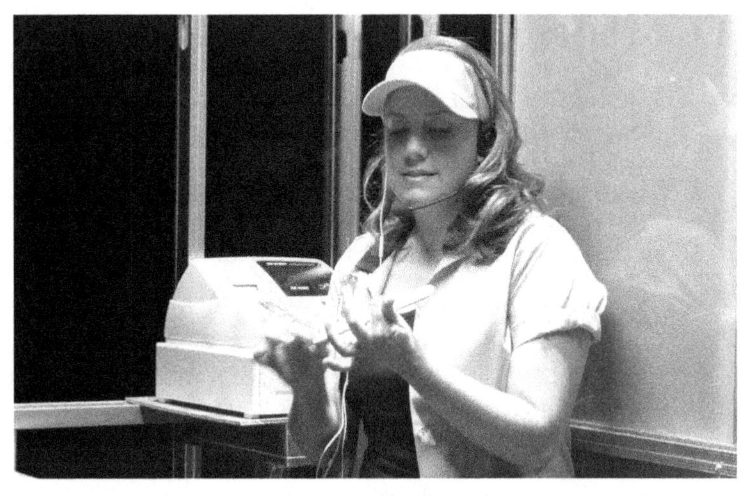

SCENE 4: Gamer

(HOURS LATER. **SOUND**: CA$$IE PLAYS SOME GAME ON HER SMARTPHONE. IT'S AN ESPECIALLY VIOLENT GAME, MAYBE *God of War II*, WHICH HAS REFERENCES TO CLASSICAL GREECE.)

CA$$IE

(FUCKING UP.) Shit! (**SOUND**: ONE OF HER MEN DIES. **SOUND**: GAME ON.) Get back here, you little fucker. Achilles!! Dude, you are so dead. You're all dead.

(**SOUND**: A BEEP AT THE DRIVE-THRU.)

(IGNORING BEEP.) Go back into your tent and plan away, Achilles. Ha! You better get your game on. OK-OK-OK-OK. Give me the beast, give me the beast, give me the beast. That's right... Come on - give me the beast, baby. YES!! Centaur! OK now help me centaur. Agh! Run! Jesus Chr...! Agh! Aghhhh!

(**SOUND**: A BEEP AT THE DRIVE-THRU.)

(IGNORING BEEP.) Whoo! Haha. OK next one, next one. What?!! *Please!*, you think you're a match for me AND the centaur? Ha! Here we go. (**SOUND**: LOTS AND LOTS OF KILLING AND DEATH.) All this blood, barrels and barrels and barrels of it! Thick purple gore, eyeballs, innards stretched around the earth six times, the mortal strings of tendons plucked and slashed by the serrated spinal columns of innocent children. Hahaha! Splintered bones like toothpicks strewn across the plain, oceans and oceans of plasma, sunken into parched lakebeds and dry fields of wheat, encasing all the artifacts of history like flies in putrid honey-amber. So friggin cool. And all this for the love of some chick. I mean, was she *that* pretty?

(**SOUND**: A BEEP AT THE DRIVE-THRU.)

Hi!, I'm Ca$$ie!!, standard-bearer of the apocalypse! May I take your order?!

(RIPS THE HEADSET OFF OF HER HEAD, THROWS IT ON THE FLOOR, RESUMES GAME. **SOUND**: GAME.)

What now? *What?!* O hell no. Ok now you're gonna pay. Hell yes, you're gonna pay.

(**SOUND**: LOUD THUD AND ELECTRONIC SOUNDSCAPE. CA$$IE IS SUDDENLY IN A WILD TRANCE.)

Water levels rising. I see the ice floe disappearing, disappearing. Skinny polar bears like rats remembering how to swim. So many hurricanes. And you've never seen such a hot, blinding hurricane. Piles of rubble where the house used to be. Strangled with seaweed. Roofs underfoot. Trunks covered with flies. Fish all gone, nothing but debris now floating rancid with mercury or boiled to death in the rivers. Fire! Fire!! Frantic butterflies seeking higher ground. Saltseawater surging ever closer, lapping the rusted spokes of your wheelchair. A bus on top of a glass building. Trees upside down.

(**SOUND**: DRIVE-THRU BEEP OVERTAKES THE SOUND OF THE GAME. **LIGHTS**: CHANGE.)

SCENE 5: Prison Workout

(CA$$IE STARTS DOING PUSH-UPS ON HER CHAIR, NOTICES HER ANKLE BRACELET, STARTS DOING LEG-LIFTS. SHE STARTS THE P90X WORKOUT, THEN SUDDENLY RUNS TO THE DRIVE-THRU WINDOW.)

CA$$IE

Get me the fuck out of here!

Help! Help me!!

Get me out of here!!!

(**SOUND**: THE DISTANT BUT URGENT NEIGH OF A BIG HORSE. CA$$IE STEPS FORWARD, CURIOUS.)

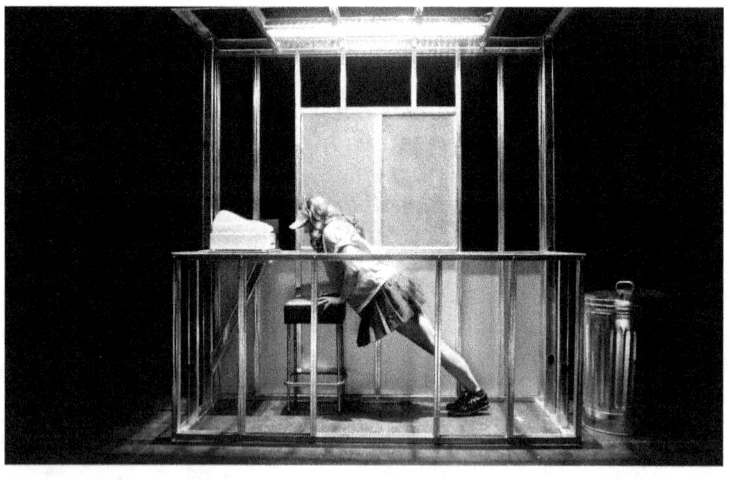

SCENE 6: A dream about a horse

(EYES CLOSED, CA$$IE KNEELS.)

CA$$IE

So tall. I have to stretch my neck and lean way back to look you in the eye. It's a glass eye, and wet. It's a black, black eight ball. So large I can see my whole body in it, tapering down down down to the floor like a rubberband girl, a girl made of saltwater taffy stretched from the boardwalk to my own mouth. I move closer. My head is distorted in that deep blackness. Closer. My face is a fish. Closer, closer. My feet are tiny stamps. We stare at each other. And stare. And wait to see who'll blink first.

(SILENCE. FINALLY.) I do. Of course I do.

(**SOUND**: WHINNY.) Sh. Shh. Why didn't we always have horses in our house? (WHISPERS.) *Why didn't we always have horses?* I wanna know how you got here and where you came from. You look like you've got a secret. So, what is it? (PAUSE.)

It's three in the morning and since you've come this far into the city down the interstate through the neighborhood past the gate into the front door without knocking up the stairs without a sound down the creaky hallway past my parents room to my bed the least you can do is open your mouth and speak. A horse that climbs stairs can surely speak. But whisper, please. I'm the only one awake right now, but... aren't there things to do? How could anybody sleep?

Somebody let you in the gate. Was it me? Oopsie!

(**SOUND**: WHINNY.) What's wrong? Did you forget who I am? Whoa! (GIGGLE.) Easy now. Nuzzler. You're a lot bigger than me so you have to be gentle. Haha, that's right. You're sweeter than my kitten, aren't you? Shhh. Did you run all the way just to see me? Aww. I knew you'd come. I knew someday, after all this fighting and all this trouble, that there would be a horse in the night. A horse indeed. I knew it! I knew you would bring yourself to my gate, like a gift, and that I would find you here. So tall.

(**SOUND**: BEEP FROM THE DRIVE-THRU.)

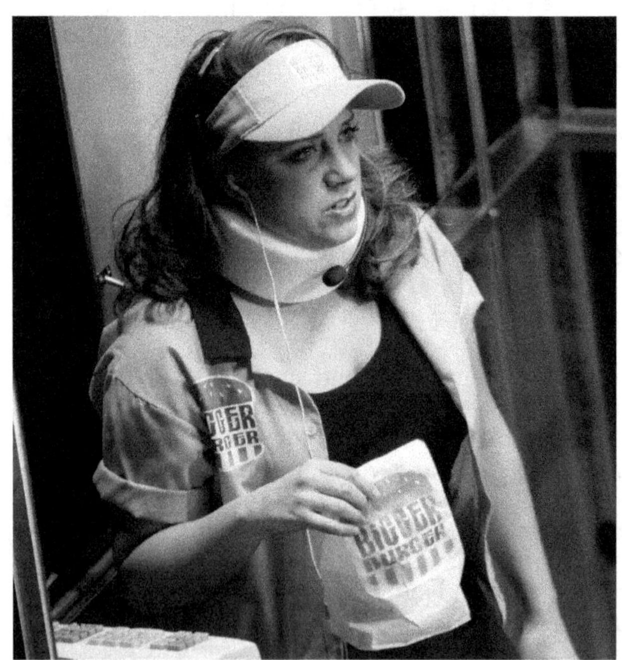

SCENE 7: my little brother

(CA$$IE AT THE DRIVE-THRU. SHE SPEAKS INTO HER HEADSET MIC.)

CA$$IE

So guess who got a 98 on the essay for *World History*? (POINTS TO HERSELF WITH BOTH THUMBS.) Dis bitch, right hurr. Ha! Essays are my favorite. Yeah, cuz if you're not 100% sure of the material you can just sorta explode words all over everything and blind them with style and detail and verbal agility. I mean, *World History*? Yawn. But you can totally make a game of it – just pretend you're, I dunno, pretend you're writing a new textbook, yeah!, and you wanna make sure future generations will read this textbook and believe that the government has always done the right thing in every tiny situation. That way they'll hold onto some modicum of pride in their country and not behave subversively or, take their savings out of the banks, or, I dunno, move away to Costa Rica or somewhere. Pretend your job is to make history into a holiday screenplay for Steven Spielberg! Or no!, pretend your job is to give the past like a gift, the best Christmas present ever, to future generations, students, who'll read this textbook and decide that it was all worth it: the building boats to sail across treacherous and vast seas, clubbing the natives in the water as you approach, hacking through the brush, killing bugs, building fires and homes and doing charitable acts and making large families and discovering cures for diseases and nuclear power and wireless internet. Now... just think for a second about what that textbook looks like, and POW, there's your essay!

GUY AT DRIVE-THRU

Um, I just wanted to order some food?

CA$$IE

This will sound totally wacko, but ever since my car accident... I've been having the freakiest dreams. I can see pictures of people I know, like my family and teachers and my friends, I can see pictures of them in my head, doing things, and then later, the next day or the next month, the things happen. Do you believe in that kinda thing? I never used to, but I'm telling you, and I don't know why I'm telling a total stranger something I've never breathed a word of before, not even to my mom, but, I'm... I'm like, a soothsayer. I'm afraid to shut my eyes. And I, God help me, I was wondering – I've got a terrible feeling right now. I dreamed last night that serpents of all colors were licking my ears, and today I'm seeing all kinds of things: briefcases and white dust, blood on the floor and plywood on the windows, chaos and rape and bills that never got paid, spray paint, AIDS and never any hope, never any cure, murder for the sake of devotion, murder on the largest scale, something or some place I don't even know sitting in rubble with feral animals nesting in plaid sofas. Will you help me? Can you help me get out of here?

(**SOUND**: CA$$IE'S PHONE RINGS.)
Shit, can you hold on a second, sir?

GUY AT DRIVE-THRU

Uh... chshh, yeah I guess.

CA$$IE

Great! Hold on just a second. (ANSWERS HER PHONE.) Hi, Mommy! Are you coming to pick me up? (PAUSE.) Mom?

HECUBA ON THE PHONE

Cassandra...

CA$$IE

Mom? Are you OK?

HECUBA ON THE PHONE

Hector is dead. (BREATHING.)

(**SOUND**: THE BEEPING YOU HEAR WHEN SOMEONE HAS LEFT A PHONE OFF THE HOOK. CA$$IE TAKES OFF HER HEADSET, PUTS HER PHONE DOWN. **SOUND**: THE DRUMLINE OF A HIGH SCHOOL BAND. **SOUND**: OUT. CA$$IE SINGS THE ANCIENT ICELANDIC LULLABY, *Vökuró*, PUSHES A ROLLING TOY HORSE ACROSS THE FLOOR.)

Bærinn minn / bærinn minn og þinn / sefur sæll í kyrrð / fellur mjöll / hljótt í húmi á jörð / grasið mitt / grasið mitt og þitt / geymir mold til vors

(English translation: My farm / my farm and yours / sleeps happily at peace / falls snow / silent at dusk on earth / my grass / my grass and yours / keeps the earth til spring)

(**SOUND**: GREEK FOLK MUSIC SOUNDSCAPE, VERY LOUD. **LIGHTS**: UP. CA$$IE DANCES TO FREE HECTOR'S SPIRIT – GREEK FOLKDANCE COMBINED WITH SECOND LINE, THE DANCE THAT TRAVELS BEHIND THE BAND AT THE JAZZ FUNERALS IN NEW ORLEANS. FINALLY, **SOUND**: OUT.)

CA$$IE

((My brother is a horse.))

(**SOUND**: APPLAUSE.)

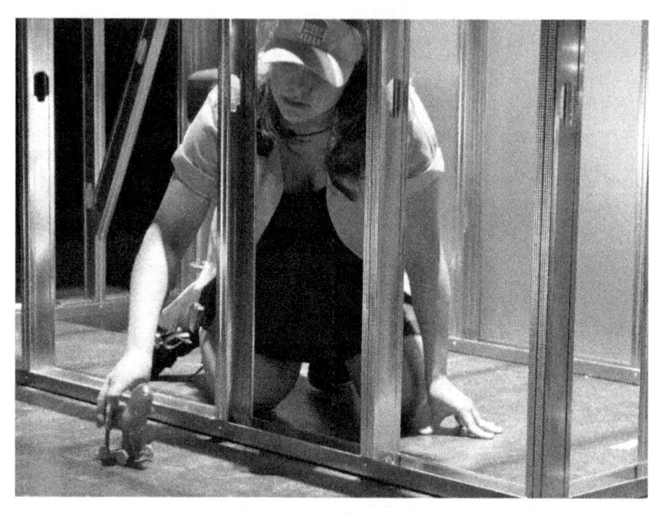

SCENE 8: Valedictory

(**SOUND**: APPLAUSE DIES. A LARGE ARENA. CA$$IE IS VERY NERVOUS AND READS HER REMARKS SELF-CONSCIOUSLY INTO A MICROPHONE.)

CA$$IE

Thank you, Principal Aeneas, for that sassy introduction.

My fellow students, faculty, administration, honored guests, parents, friends, and those who may have gotten lost looking for the pharmaceutical convention: I would first like to congratulate all of you, not just the graduating seniors, but everyone here today. We graduates can't thank you enough, and we share our success with you.

I can't say I was surprised when I found out I was Troy High School's valedictorian this year. Not to be stuck up, but it's been a neck-and-neck race since elementary school with Alexander and me, and we and our parents have been tracking every grade point for a lot of years, so we both knew exactly where we would stand at the end of this last semester. I'd like to say this to Alexander tonight – you are awesome, boy. Don't ever change.

You and Heph are sooo cute together, and I'm so glad you'll be attending prom this year as a couple. It's just my luck that the two cutest guys at Troy High School are into each other, but you have nothing but success and happiness in your future.

(**SOUND**: THUD + ELECTRONIC SOUNDSCAPE.)

I can see it: *a tower the most gorgeous many stories high two hundred and forty ships with golden prows many many armed soldiers look out for you red banners golden wreaths gold gold all in gold gold lions bulls and soaring eagles and light, light, light the lights. burning all night. the golden ring. the sirens who sing.*

(**SOUND**: OUT. SHE REGAINS COMPOSURE.)

High school is a magical time. A time when we discover at last who we are, what our values are, and embark on a journey that will lead us who-knows-where. It's appropriate at this time to offer our heartfelt thanks to the wonderful teachers who have gotten us to where we are today. I know my fellow seniors would join me in especially thanking our beloved Dr. Apollo who, of course, isn't here tonight. We wish you all the best in whatever you do, Dr. Apollo, and we hope that whatever road you're walking down is leading you to Rome.

I mention Dr. Apollo not only because he is an excellent educator, but because he abruptly disappeared after many years of service to this school and its students. We were never told why. Could it have something to do with the fact that Apollo had a PhD and therefore commanded a higher salary than most of his colleagues, and that school system budgets and teacher salaries across the country have been severely cut in the last decade as we struggle to fund the imperialistic wars we're waging in the far corners of the earth? Perhaps. At any rate, thank you, teachers. Though you be scattered by the four winds, we will remember you.

And I'll always remember my best friends on the cheerleading squad – Helen, Aphra, Penny, Iris and

Pandora – and how amazed we were that we won Nationals three years in a row (*Go Troy! Love you girls!*), the senior trip to New York, the choir concert, going to state in volleyball, and so many wonderful memories that will be with me forever. I encourage my fellow seniors to follow their dreams, to choose a career that will bring them joy, and to remember that the number of zeros on that paycheck will be directly proportionate to how bad you wanted it.

On a more personal note, I'd like to ask each parent, family member and friend here today to stay in our lives. We'll need your advice and wisdom as we move forward and attempt to find our way in a big and frightening world. We'll need to know that you've got our backs no matter what, and that we can call on you if times get tough.

(**SOUND**: A CELL PHONE RINGS IN THE CROWD.)

Hahaa! I'll wrap this up.

In closing, I'd just like to once again say Thank you, Troy. Thank you, Troy High School, HOME OF THE FIGHTING TROJANS!!! Woo-Hoo! And I'd like to ask each of you to take a good hard look and remember us: (SHE STEPS OUT.)

We are your future.

(**SOUND**: POLICE SIREN WINDING DOWN.
LIGHTS: CHANGE.)

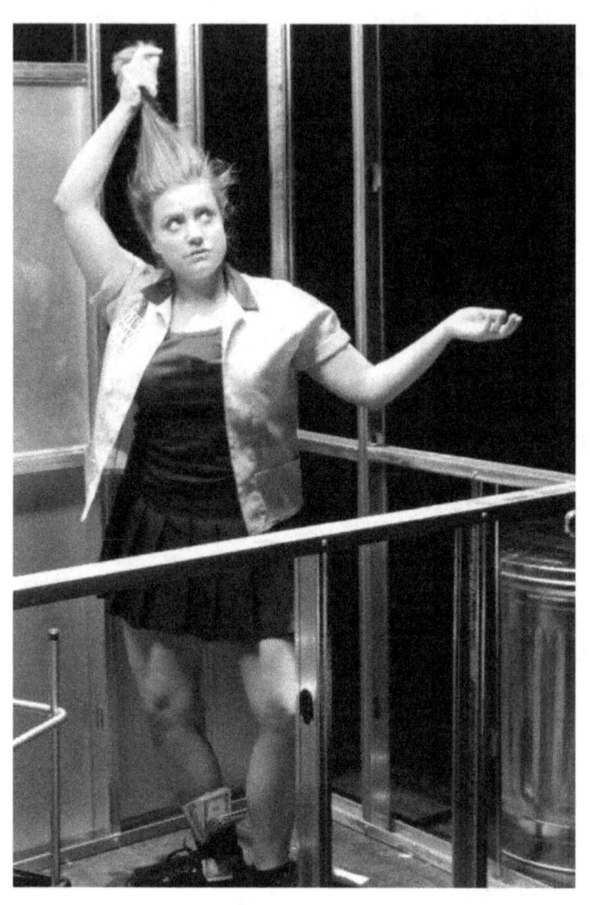

SCENE 9: Mugshot

(THAT FATEFUL NIGHT LAST WEEK. CA$$IE IS SNOT-FLYING DRUNK. SHE HOLDS A SIGN THAT SAYS: TPD – Cassandra – 493022. **SOUND**: DRUNK TANK AMBIENCE.)

CA$$IE

Wha? I'm under arrest? No, I'm the Easter Bunny. Hahaa!

Excuse me, sir? *Officer!* Hey, officer... So one day, the mother superior calls all the nuns into the chapel and says, "Sisters, I have an announcement to make: I've got a case of gonorrhea." A hush falls across the room. Finally a little nun stands up in the back and says, "Hallelujah! I'm so sick of the chardonnay!" Hahaa!

Hey, where're my friends? Hey, Aphra! Where's my brotherrr?! (WHISPERS.) Hey, officer. My bra is drunk tank pink. I said, *My bra is drunk tank pink!* Isn't that awesome? Hahaha! (BEAT.) The right to remain silent. O right, right. (SHE HOLDS UP THE SIGN. **LIGHTS**: CAMERA FLASH.) So retarded. Doesn't everyone have the right to remain silent? That's pretty much the only right we actually honest-to-God frigging have, to remain silent. I mean really. People don't really wanna hear your opinion anyway. They don't wanna know what's *really* going on, you know? People don't really care how your day was or what you had for lunch. People just want peace and quiet so they can trust the government and be happy without any of your annoying distractions of fact and reality. Tell people the truth and they think you're crazy.

(CA$$IE TURNS TO PROFILE; **LIGHTS**: FLASH.)

CA$$IE as the OFFICER
You have the right to remain silent.

CA$$IE
O, really?

CA$$IE as the OFFICER
That's right.

CA$$IE
That'd work out great for you, wouldn't it?

CA$$IE as the OFFICER
"I beg your pardon?"

CA$$IE
(SHOUTS.) IF I REMAINED SILENT!! Yeah, you'd like me to remain silent. You'd like that because you're gonna be in some hot frigging water when my parents find out about this. I mean, excuse me, do you know who I am? Do you know who my father is? Any idea? Lemme give you a hint: I'm Cassandra, you moron! CASSANDRA!! There's gonna be a shit storm of apocalyptic proportion in about 3 seconds and you're gonna wish to hell you'd listened to me. (BEAT.) But yeah, I'll remain silent. No problem.

CA$$IE as the OFFICER
"Index finger, please."

CA$$IE
Hm, let's see... How bout I give you *this* one instead? (FLIPS HIM OFF. **SOUND**: TIRES SCREECHING + A TERRIBLE CAR ACCIDENT. **LIGHTS**: BLACKOUT.)

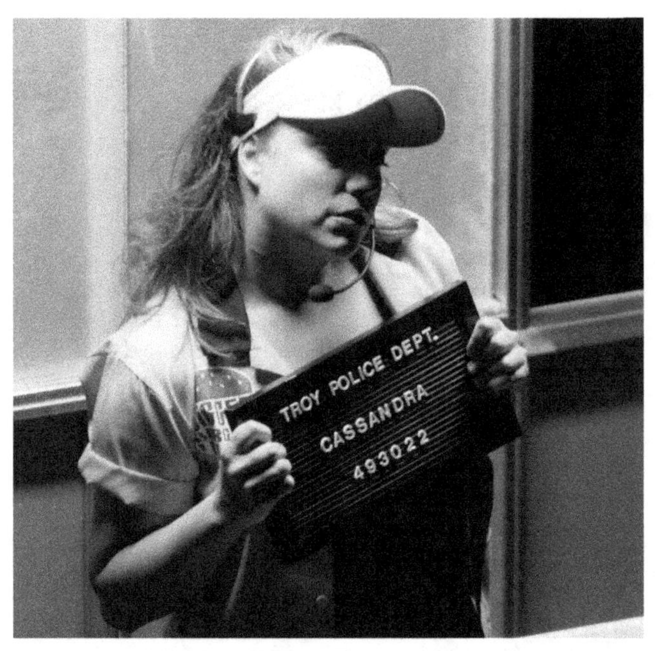
TROY POLICE DEPT.
CASSANDRA
493022

SCENE 10: Snow tastes like minutes

(**SOUND**: A MUSIC BOX MADE OF ICICLES. CA$$IE IS ASLEEP.)

CA$$IE

I'm skating on the river in Grandpa's tattered coat we found in the attic. The river is long and narrow with steep cliffs on either side. A silver ribbon undulating rolling. Silence, my breath, my skates scraping the ice. You can skate for hours and hours, for days even, without stopping or seeing another living creature. You lose track of time because there are no markers, no signposts, no points on the landscape to remind you where you are. Nothing occurs to you but to go forward. Push ahead. Hope for the best. Today it snows so hard I can't see. Big, opaque flakes of snow that obscure everything. So much of it. Not gentle snow, but urgent, silent snow. An army of it. Where is everyone? (PAUSE.) This snow tastes like minutes. Little shards on my tongue, sharp and frozen. So many of them. So many minutes that I can't see the river, the cliffs, the ice. So much ice. So much snow that I can't see anything, not even my breath. So I just skate and skate and skate through the minutes and across the vast continent that's frozen. I don't worry: I'm leaving marks, tracks on the ice. See there? So if I should get lost they can follow those tracks – long slices in the ice – and find me. That is, as long as the snow doesn't cover them all up.

(**SOUND:** OUT.)

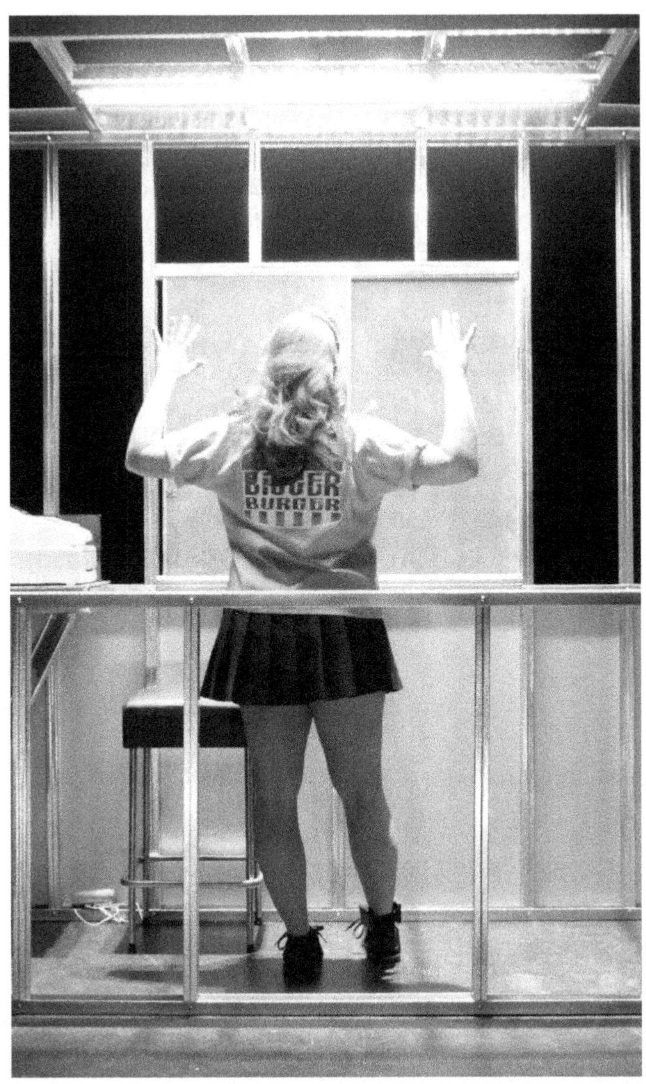
BIGGER
BURGER

SCENE 11: I told you

(**SOUND**: INSANE TAMMY WYNETTE SOUNDSCAPE. CA$$IE SUDDENLY THROWS HER VISOR ASIDE WITH A SCREAM AND STARTS MANIACALLY STYLING HER HAIR, ALMOST AS IF SHE WOULD RIP IT OUT. **SOUND**: ANOTHER DRIVE-THRU BEEP.)

CA$$IE

(INTO HEADSET MIC:) Welcome to Bigger Burger, order whenever you're ready. (PAUSE.) Hello?

VOICE WITH GERMAN ACCENT

Ja, ja. I don't know what I'm having.

CA$$IE

(STIFLING A LAUGH:) Order whenever you're ready, sir.

VOICE WITH GERMAN ACCENT

Eh, hallo?

CA$$IE

Yes, yes, I'm here, sir. Order whenever you're ready.

VOICE WITH GERMAN ACCENT

No system based on greed can continue forever.

CA$$IE

I beg your pardon?

VOICE WITH GERMAN ACCENT

I told you over and over: People are not commodities. Workers are not machines.

CA$$IE

Karl Marx???

VOICE WITH GERMAN ACCENT
Hallo, Ca$$ie.

CA$$IE
Dude, I can't believe you're at the Bigger Burger! HaHa! Holy Shit!! I've been studying your work all semester with "Who-wants-to-swallow" Apollo. Wow! Like, I never like, talked to a celebrity before, even through a headset. Shit! Pull up – can you, can I like, get a picture with you?

VOICE WITH GERMAN ACCENT
You should get out of here.

CA$$IE
What? It'll just take a second.

VOICE WITH GERMAN ACCENT
You should get out of here.

CA$$IE
What? What do you mean?

VOICE WITH GERMAN ACCENT
Go now, Ca$$ie. I'm not joking about this.

CA$$IE
Believe me, I would if I could. I'm on probation and I have an ankle bra-

VOICE WITH GERMAN ACCENT
But I was right! It took a century of foolish mistakes to see it, but I was right after all. The markets have imploded, and the banks are all closed. The cities are burning east to west, one by one. It's the end of the empire, Ca$$ie, just as I said it would be. All the

executives and government officials have already left for Costa Rica.

CA$$IE

(HORRIFIED.) *Are you shitting me?* (BEAT. THOROUGHLY CONFUSED.) Wait, could you repeat that, please?

VOICE WITH GERMAN ACCENT

You should get out of here. It's very quiet now, but soon there'll be blood in the streets. I told you it would only be a matter of time. Do as I say and leave right now, Ca$$ie.

CA$$IE

But I can't! I've got an ankle bracelet! (PAUSE.) Karl?

VOICE WITH GERMAN ACCENT

What happens always happens, Ca$$ie.

CA$$IE

Karl!

Wait, Karl!!!

(SHE FRANTICALLY PUSHES BUTTONS. **SOUNDSCAPE**: THROUGH THE DRIVE-THRU SPEAKER, KARL MARX IS SINGING *O, My Darling Clementine*, ACCOMPANIED BY A DEMENTED ACCORDION THAT'S PLAYING A DIFFERENT SONG, FOOTSTEPS IN A HALLWAY, A CHILD IN THE BATHTUB, A TOASTER, AND WOLVES.)

(CA$$IE TAKES OFF HEADSET AND BACKS AWAY FROM REGISTER, RECITES *Communist Manifesto.* SHE STARTS DANCING TO THE MUSIC, RETREATING MORE AND MORE INTO MADNESS. SHE TAKES ALL THE MONEY FROM THE

REGISTER AND HIDES IT IN HER CLOTHING, RECITING WIKIPEDIA ENTRY FOR NEW YORK STOCK EXCHANGE, THEN RESUMES STYLING HER HAIR. SHE PULLS HER LONG HAIR OVER HER HEAD AND WHIRLS LIKE A DERVISH.)

(**SOUND**: A BOMB HITS CLOSE TO THE BIGGER BURGER, MUSIC OUT. CA$$IE STOPS. **SOUND**: ANOTHER BOMB. CA$$IE TAKES COVER.)

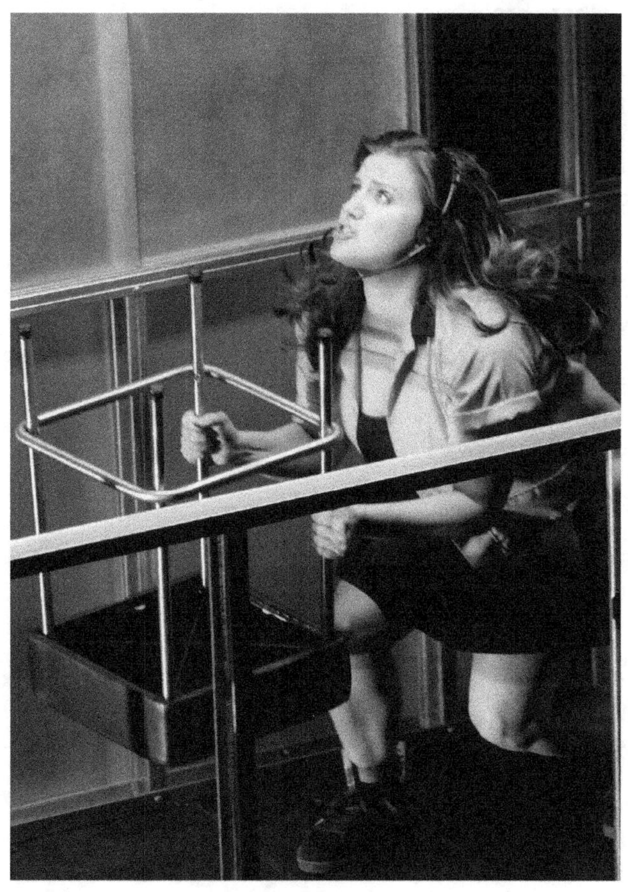

EPILOGUE: Cry

(**SOUND**: IN THE DISTANCE, A HORSE RUNS PAST. CA$$IE IS COMPLETELY DERANGED AND HUDDLED UNDER THE REGISTER IN THE WINDOW OF THE DRIVE-THRU.)

CA$$IE

Mother, let them take me
Let them break me in half
Shh
Let them dishonor every word we ever spoke to each other
You, my father, Hector, all of us
Let them try to destroy us
Reorganize us
Colonize us

(**SOUND**: GUNFIRE, EXPLOSIONS APPROACHING.)

Let them use me
Violate me
Throw me on the back of a horse and sweep me into a starless night
Don't weep
Don't look with sad eyes

I will have a crown
I will have diamonds
And velvet gown
From cloud-capped towers with gilded domes
I'll look down on the tops of tall orange trees
My subjects like ants on the ground

(**LIGHTS**: POWER BLINKS OUT; CA$$IES IS LIT ONLY BY EMERGENCY LIGHTS. THE WAY CA$$IE IS WEARING HER VISOR UPSIDE-DOWN, AND

WITH THE LARGE EMERGENCY FLASHLIGHT IN HER HAND, SHE LOOKS LIKE A TWISTED VERSION OF THE STATUE OF LIBERTY. **SOUND**: GUNFIRE, EXPLOSIONS, SOLDIERS MARCHING, WOMEN SCREAMING, CHILDREN CRYING, GLASS BREAKING, ETC., BUILDS.)

Let me be queen, Mother
And let them cry when they see the monster I've become
Cry when I come crashing down like the Colossus at Rhodes
Cry when the seas swell and then roar and smash back together, finally meeting at the point where I stood for a moment:

The new used-to-be! I am Rome! I am Persia! I am Britain, Byzantium, (BEGINS TO WEEP.) I am Troy! So, cry.

(CA$$IE THROWS BIGGER BURGER BAGS OUT THE WINDOW OF THE DRIVE-THRU.)

Cry-y-y-y-y! Cry-y-y-y-y-y-y! CRY!!

(CA$$IE PUTS ON A SMILE AND CHEERS TO A BLARING TECHNO VERISON OF THE CHINESE NATIONAL ANTHEM.)

(**LIGHTS**: ALL OUT BUT CA$$IE'S FLASHLIGHT, WHICH WHIRLS IN THE DARKNESS. FINALLY...)

(**LIGHTS**: OUT.)

END OF PLAY

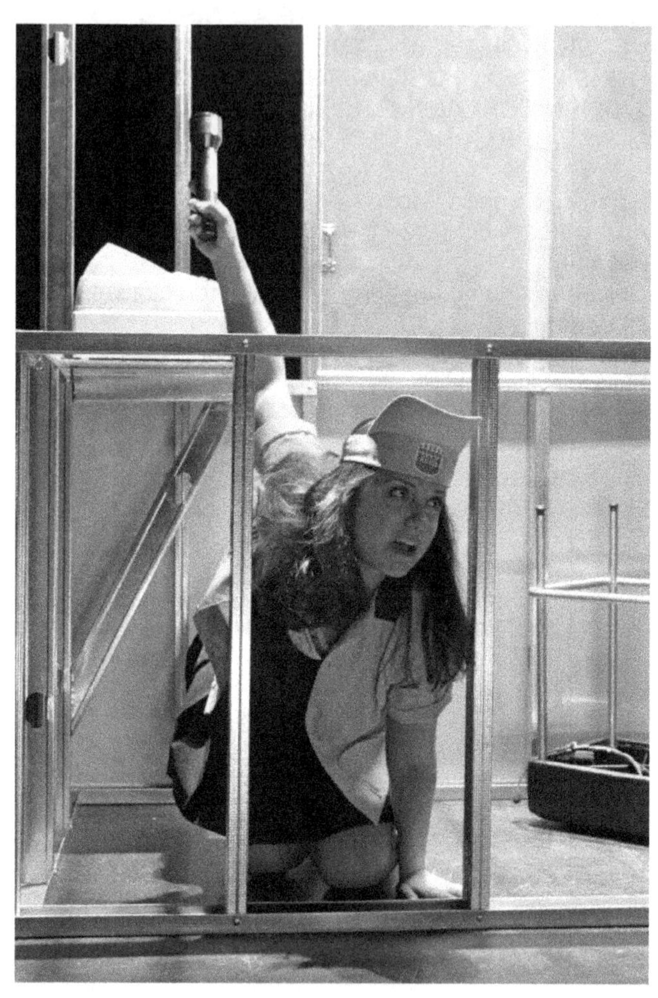

www.ingramcontent.com/pod-product-compliance
Lightning Source LLC
LaVergne TN
LVHW010546100826
845148LV00013B/2629

* 9 7 8 0 6 1 5 5 9 6 9 9 0 *